ALISON WIN
PRAYERS
For Little People

Some families are very big,
Some families are small,
Some people have no family,
No family at all.

But they, like everyone, can be
Part of God's loving family;
And every one of us can share
The comfort of His loving care.

A friend is a special person
And a special thing to be,
And when my friends come calling
They sometimes stay for tea.

I choose for them my favourite toys
And share them cheerfully,
And hope that other girls and boys
Will take good care of me.

Dear Jesus,
Help me share my day
With special friends with whom I play.

Thank you, God, for eyes to see
Crimson cherries on the tree.
Thank you, God, for ears to hear
Blackbirds singing sweet and clear.
Thank you, too, that I can smell
And taste the food I eat as well;
Seeing, hearing, smell and touch
Show me of your world so much.
Help me to remember, please,
That you gave me all of these.

Thank you, God, for things that grow
    Silently beneath the snow;
    Buds their flowers safely hide,
Waiting through the wintertide.

Thank you for the sunshine, Lord,
Thank you for the spring;
For crocuses and daffodils,
The song that thrushes sing.

Thank you for the soft, green grass,
    Blossom on the trees;
    How I wish that everyone
Could see and hear all these!

Graces

All good gifts around us
Are sent from heaven above;
Then thank the Lord,
O thank the Lord,
For all his love.

For the food we eat,
And those who prepare it;
For health to enjoy it,
And friends to share it,
We thank you, O Lord.

For each refreshing drink
And every tasty plateful,
Let us stop to think
And be truly grateful.

Thank you for the world so sweet,
Thank you for the food we eat,
Thank you for the birds that sing,
Thank you, God, for everything.

Walking in the garden,
I found a wiggly worm;
I put him in a matchbox
To keep him safe from harm.
I offered him some tiny leaves –
He didn't eat them, though.
I could see he wasn't happy
And so I let him go.

I'll say a little prayer today,
For creatures great and small;
Because I know that you, dear Lord,
Made them all.

I've put some fish in Pussy's dish,
I've given her some milk.
I've gently stroked her furry coat –
It's warm, and soft as silk.
I've put a cushion by the fire
Beside my little chair.
I like to watch her lie asleep,
And listen to her purr.
Help me to remember, Lord,
In case I should forget,
To feed my pet.

Whenever, whenever we go to the sea –
Mummy and Daddy and Teddy and me –
The sea looks enormously grand.
The sea-shore seems to go on and on,
And playing in sunshine is always such fun,
So we dig and we dig in the sand.

Dear God, tonight I say thank you,
For giving me so much to do,
For all the treasures to be found
In plenty, if we look around.

Whenever, whenever we go to the sea
We build a sand castle that's bigger than me –
Sometimes we sit Teddy on top.

I'm not at all sure that he likes being there –
He gets sand in his eyes and his ears and his fur.
He'd much rather sit in my lap.

Dear Jesus, I would like to say
Thank you for my holiday.

Thank you, Lord,
   For the sea and the sand,
For holidays and outings,
And for all our fun!

There are small boats and tall boats
   A-sailing on the sea,
   And lots of little rowing boats
Bobbing merrily.

God who made the grass,
The flower, the fruit, the tree,
The day and night to pass,
Cares for me.

Tonight, dear Lord, I'd like to pray
For all the people that I love,
But who live far away.
Tonight with them my thoughts I share,
Please keep them in your loving care,
Each night and every day.

In the morning light I see
shimmering, the willow tree.
See its branches swirl and sway,
Cool and green and grey.

In the dark it stirs the air,
Shaking like a witch's hair.
I don't know why the willow tree
At night-time frightens me.

For God made all the things I see,
He even made my willow tree,
And when the night turns into day,
He'll blow that witch away!

Little diamond,
Little star,
Shining in the night.
I know that you will disappear
As soon as it is light.

Gentle Jesus,
Gentle friend,
You are always near.
And your love that knows no end
Will never disappear.

Gentle Lord, my prayers I bring;
Tonight I want to say,
Thank you, God, for everything –
We've had a lovely day!

First we pulled out the weeds,
Then we planted some seeds –
They were slippery, smooth, dry and small.
Could something so tiny
Ever grow flowers at all?

There wasn't a sound
From the bare, cold ground,
As we watched through long, silent hours;
Then our seeds, one by one,
Grew right up towards the sun,
And burst into huge, yellow flowers!

We thank you, God, for earth and sky,
And for the seeds we sow,
For sun and rain, and all good things
You send to make them grow.

Jill has a triangle,
Johnny rings a bell,
Katie shakes a tambourine,
So does Annabel.
James claps the cymbals
(One in each hand),
Charles is the drummer –
But I lead the band.

Thank you, Lord, for the people who
Make merry music wherever they go.

Tonight my prayers are for the sake
   Of all the people who
   Have always to remain awake
And work the whole night through:
   Train drivers,
   Truck drivers,
   Doctors and nurses,
   Postmen, policemen,
   And those who drive buses,
   Farmers on hills,
   Helping lambs to be born.
Bless them, dear Jesus,
And keep them from harm.

The Christ Child lay
On a bed of hay,
And a thousand stars looked down;
And the Angels sang of peace and joy,
For the Holy Child,
The Baby Boy,
For the King without a Crown.

Away in a Manger
No crib for a bed,
The little Lord Jesus
Laid down his sweet head.

The stars in the bright sky
Looked down where He lay,
The little Lord Jesus,
Asleep on the hay.

The Lord's Prayer

*Our Father
Who art in Heaven;
Hallowed be thy name;
Thy Kingdom come;
Thy will be done;
On earth as it is in Heaven.
Give us this day our daily bread,
And forgive us our trespasses,
As we forgive those who trespass against us.
And lead us not into temptation,
But deliver us from evil,
For Thine is the kingdom, the power
And the glory,
For ever and ever,
Amen.*